NOTES FOR FRIENDS   ALONG COLORADO ROADS

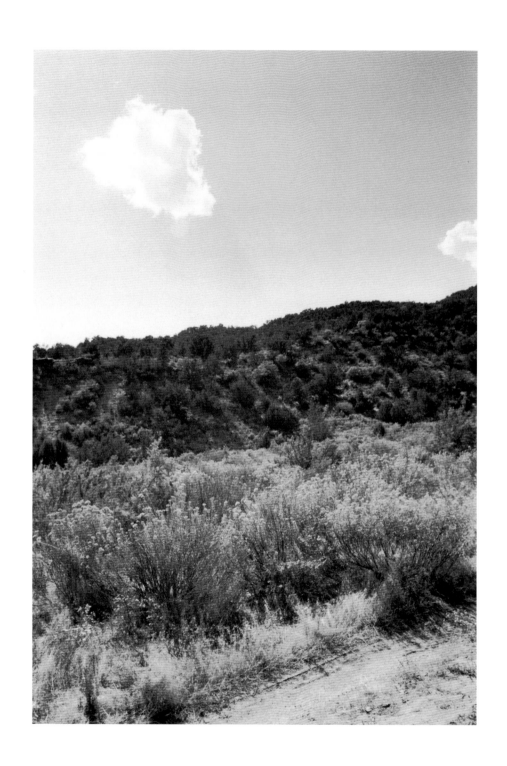

notes for friends ALONG COLORADO ROADS

Robert Adams

CENTER OF THE AMERICAN WEST   UNIVERSITY PRESS OF COLORADO

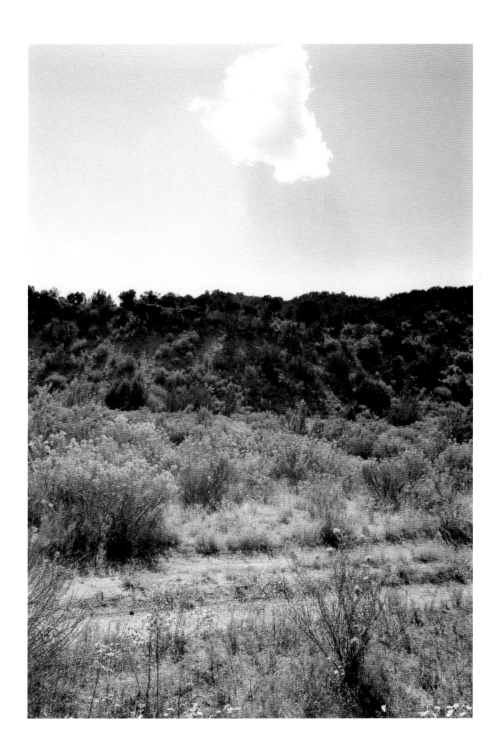

Among my favorite poems by William Stafford is one in which he endorses close observation.

Places That Will Be Saved

Sacred for what's not yet done
a little rock rolls down
maybe by a road in the woods.
I watch for them—something is
a little strange, but nothing
happens but waiting, and then
this one event: I stand there, breathing.
Sometimes a touch of wind
passes ahead of time
when the rock rolls down.
The world and I go on.

Sometime the truth will come.

We hope to see the world as it is, and by that to discover another. Because, as the poet wrote in *Old Man by the Road*,

There is no rock on the mountain
so still as the dreams I dream.

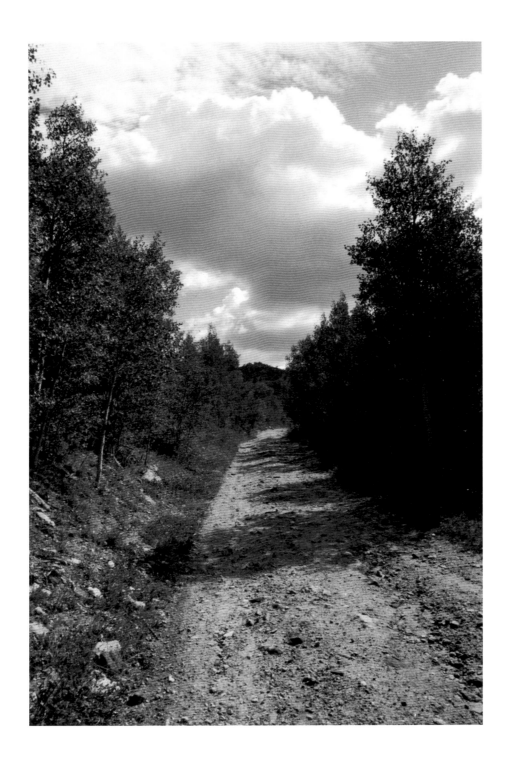

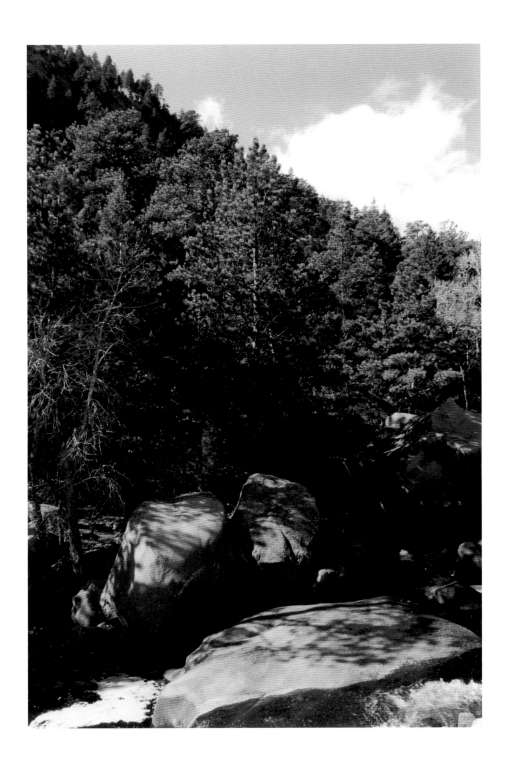

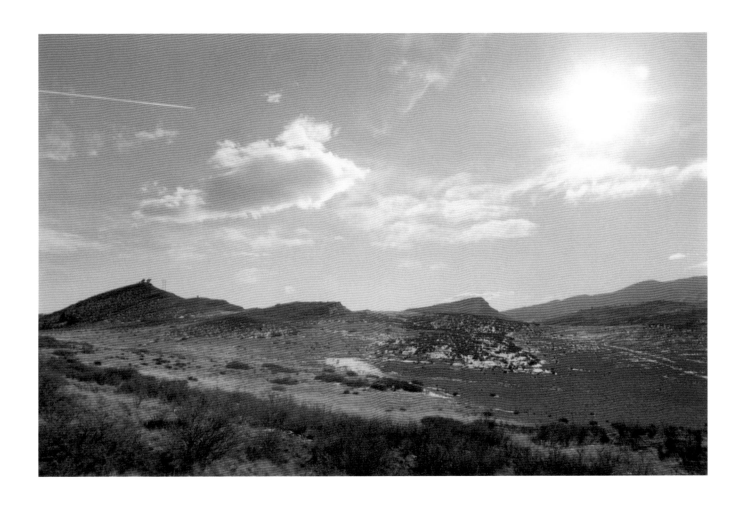

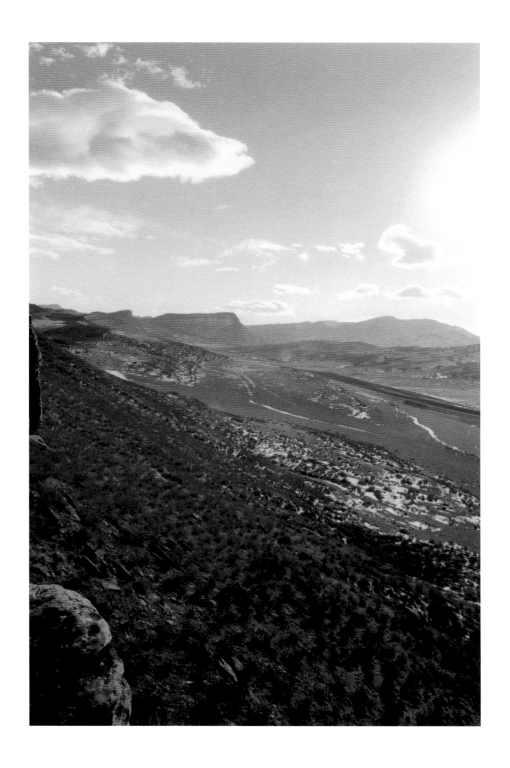

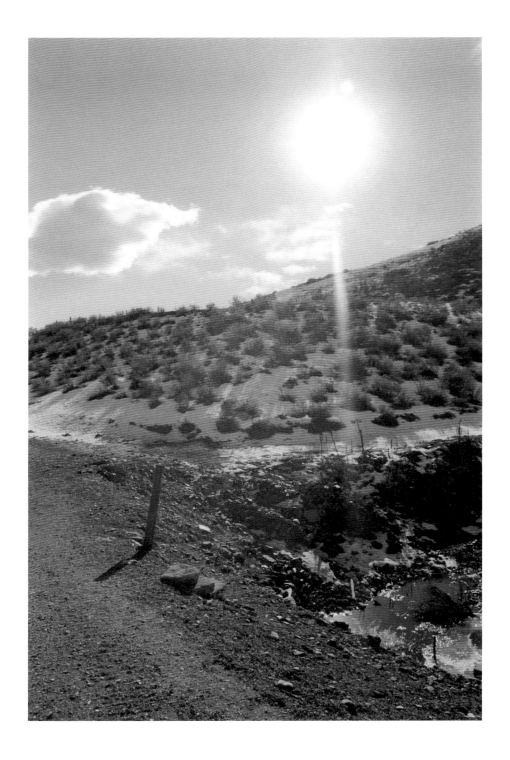

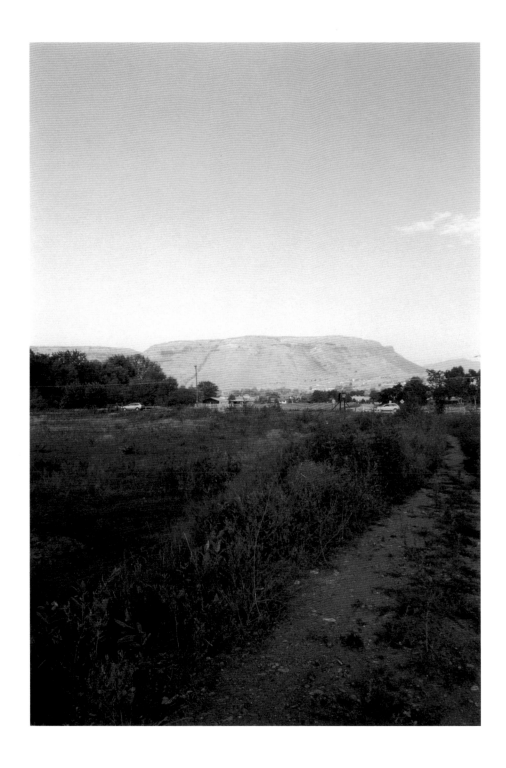

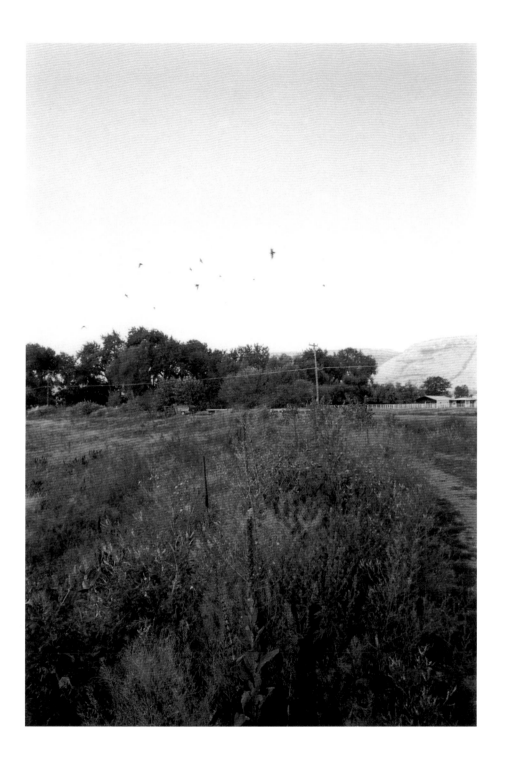

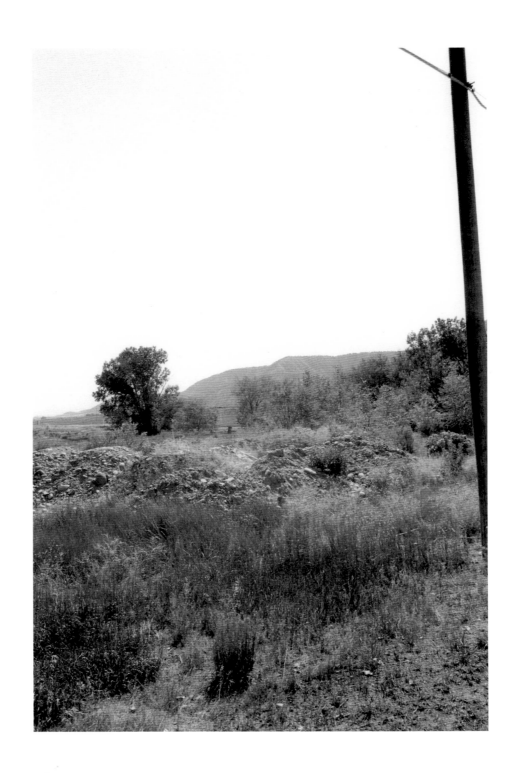

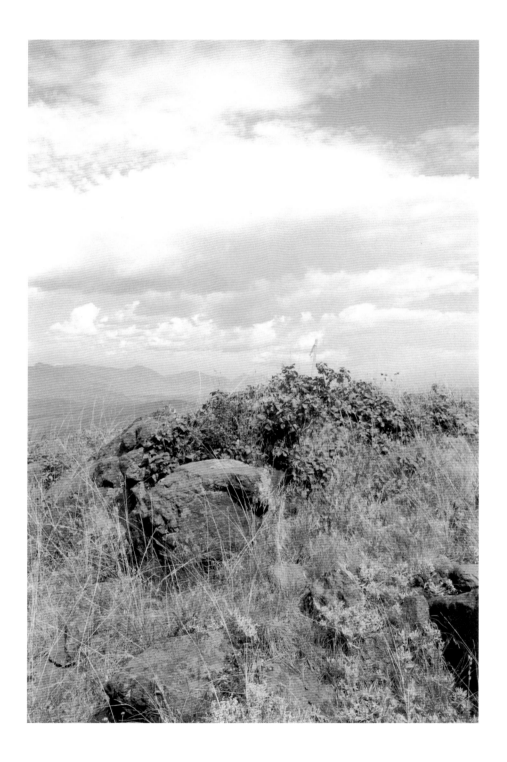

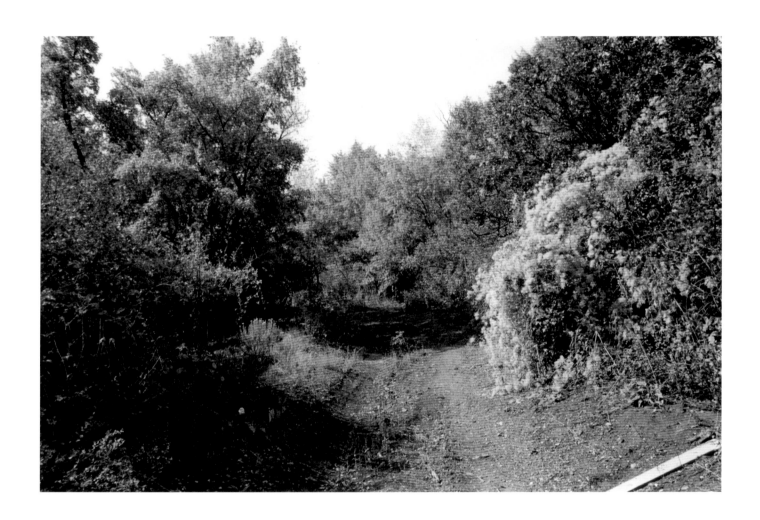

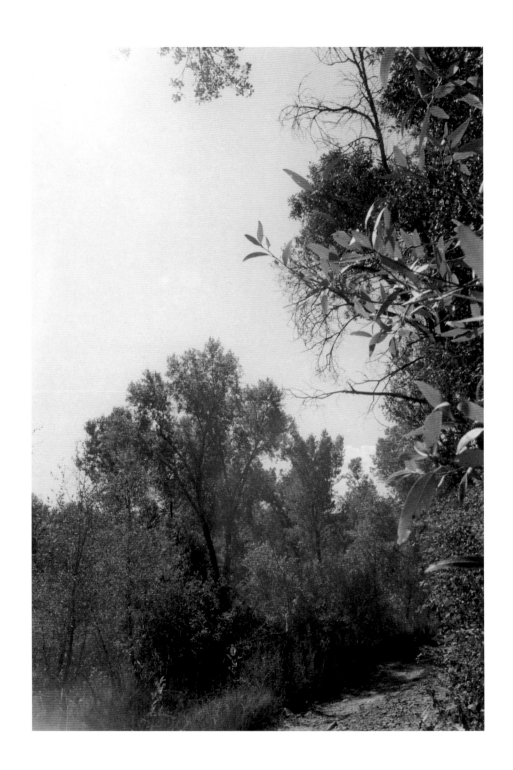

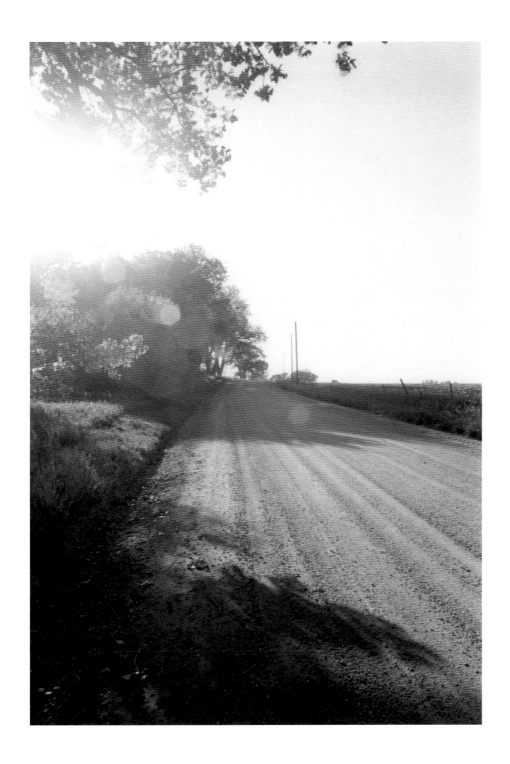

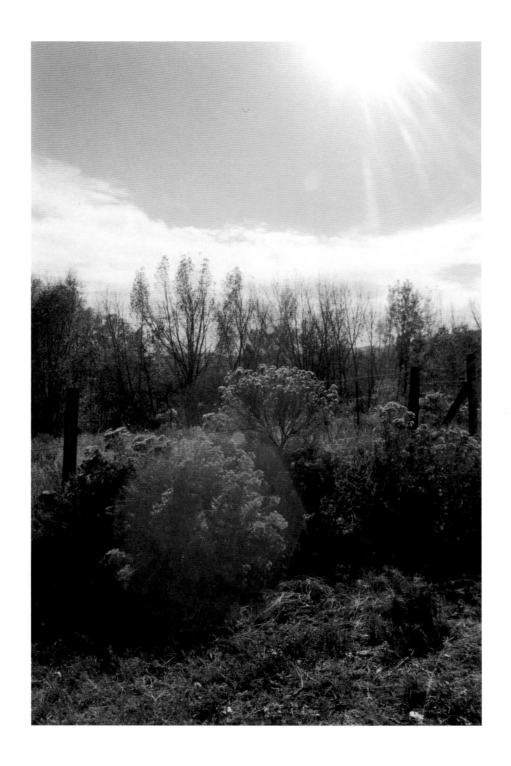

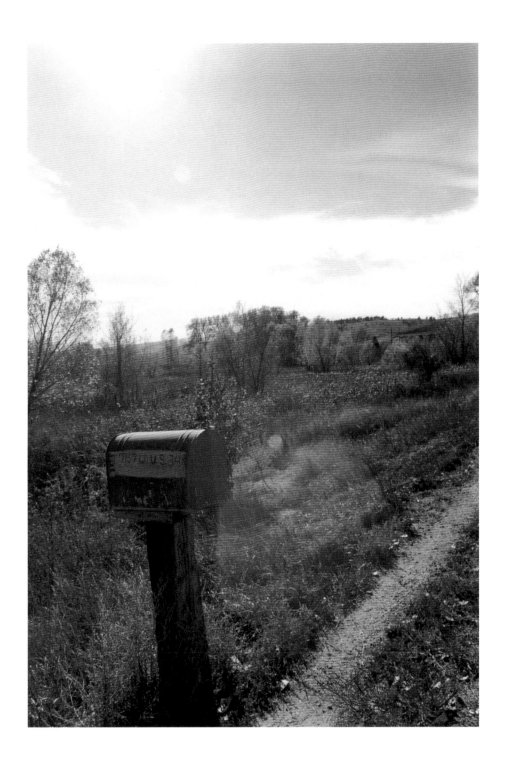

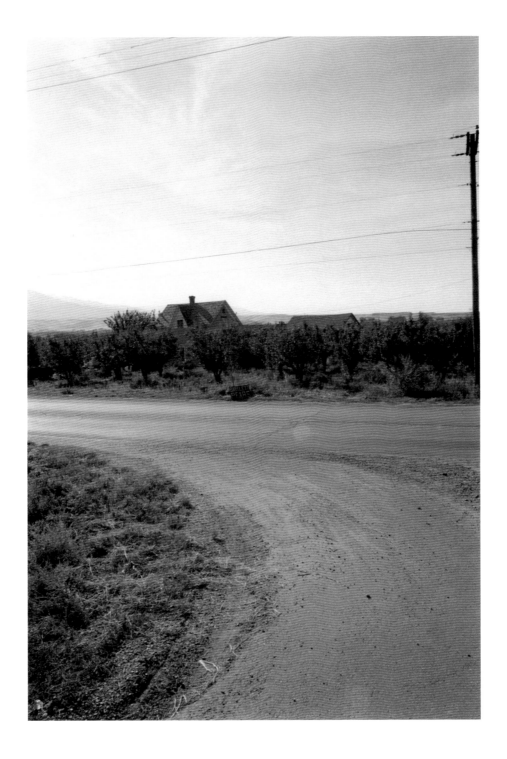

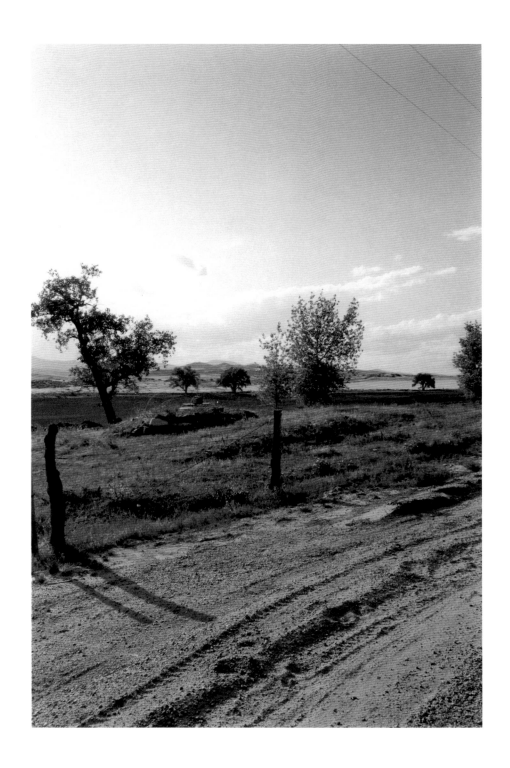

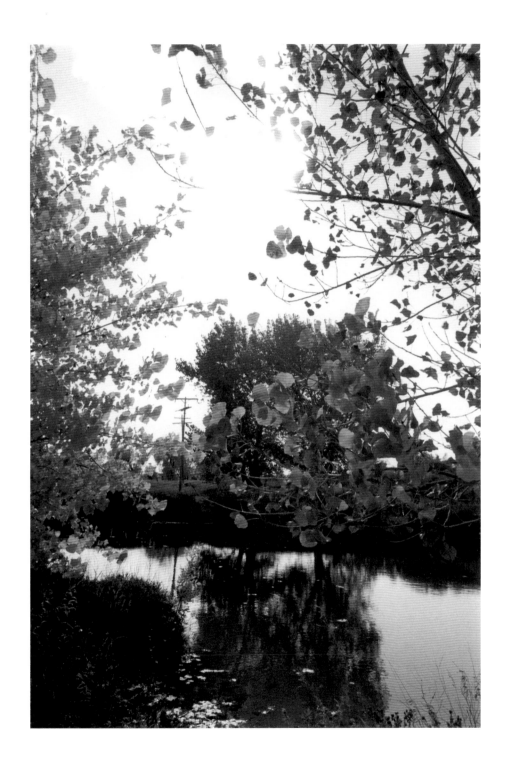

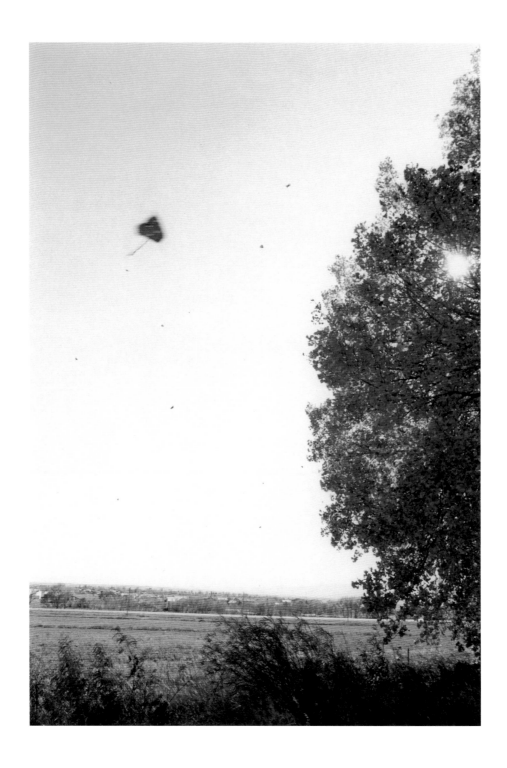

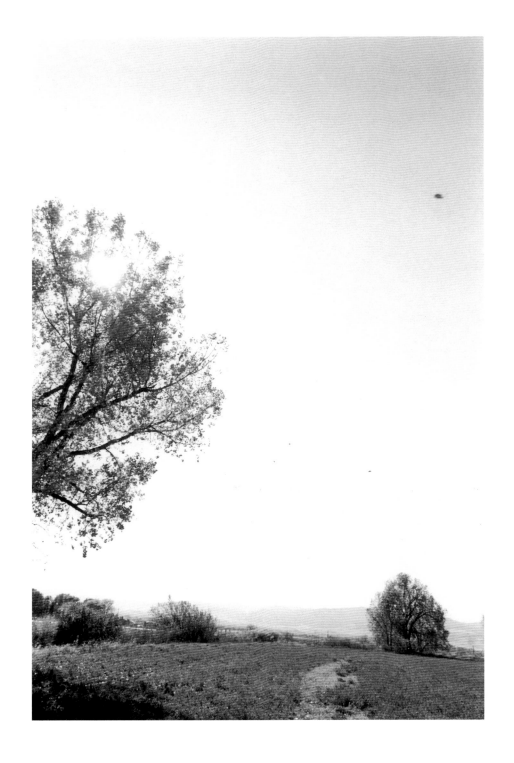

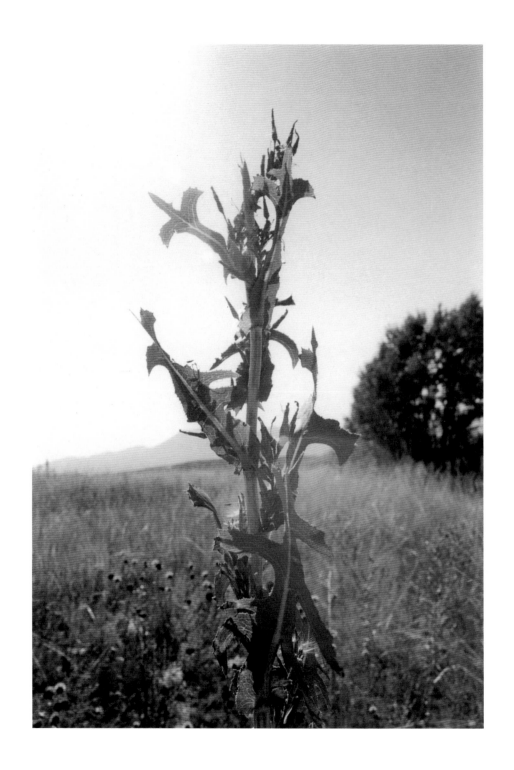

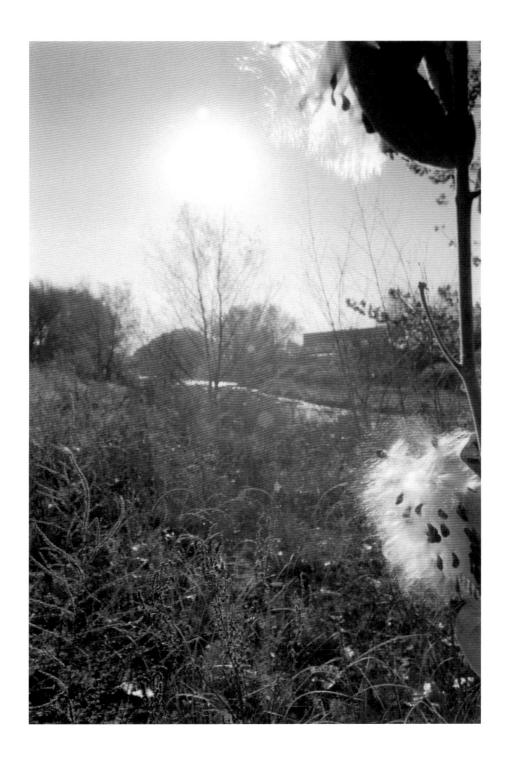

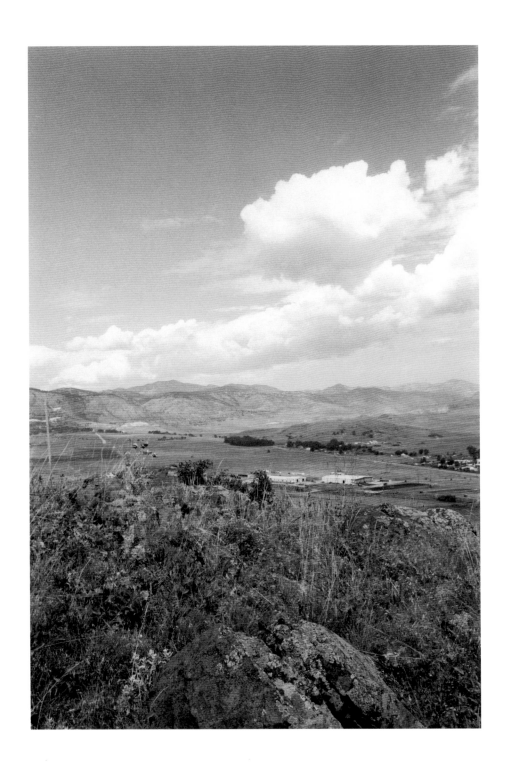

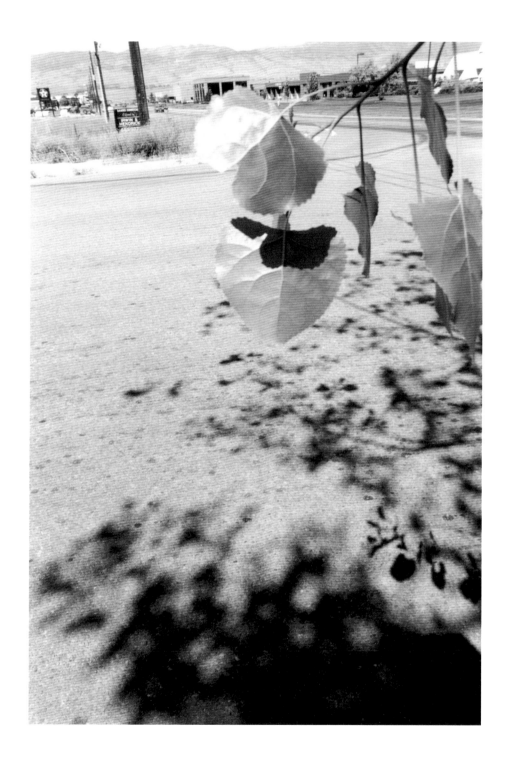

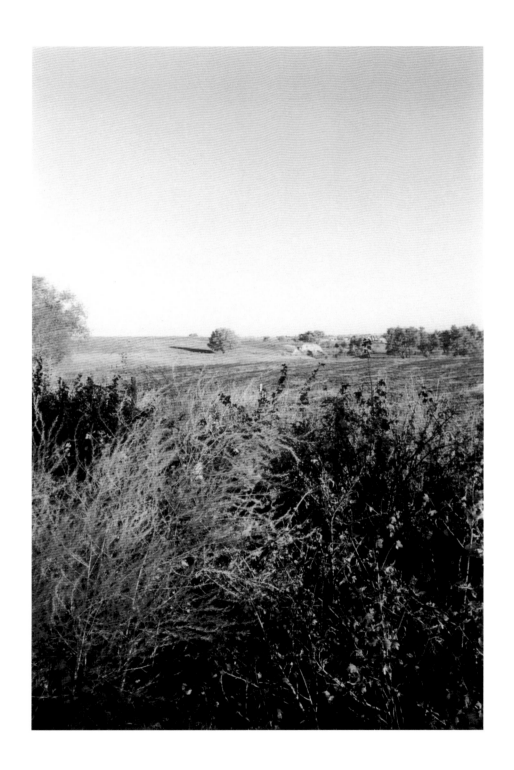

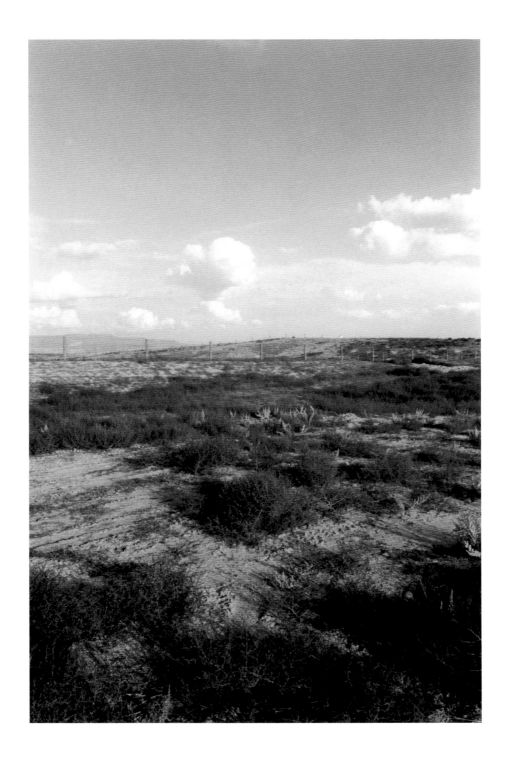

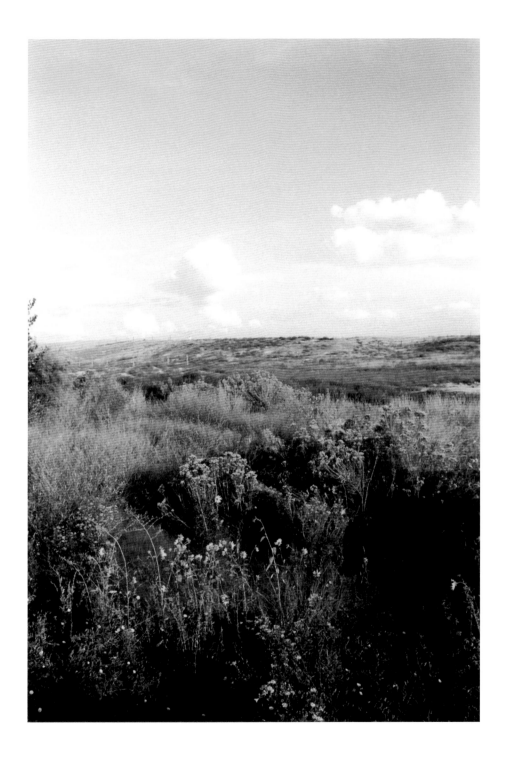

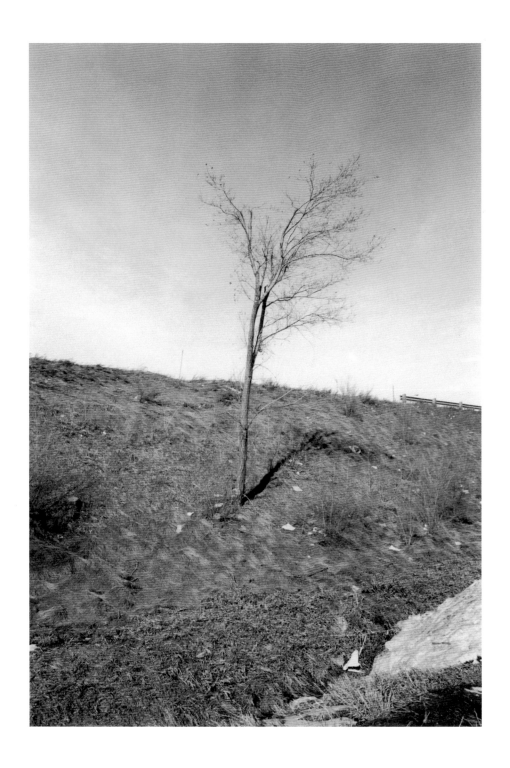

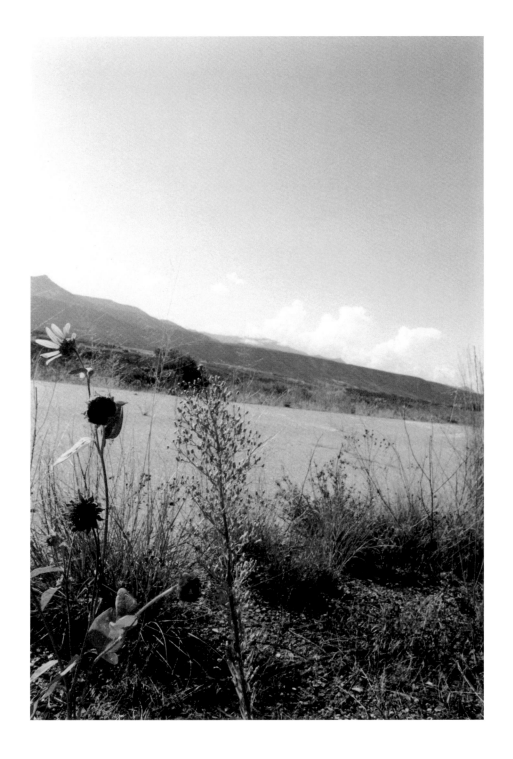

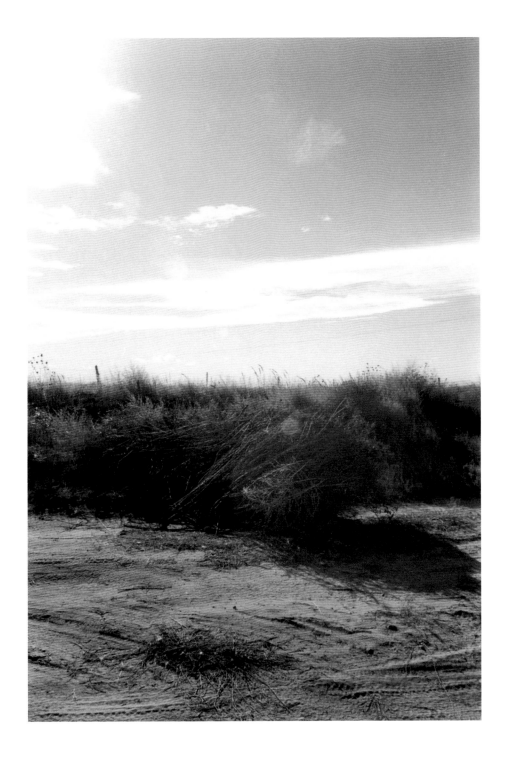

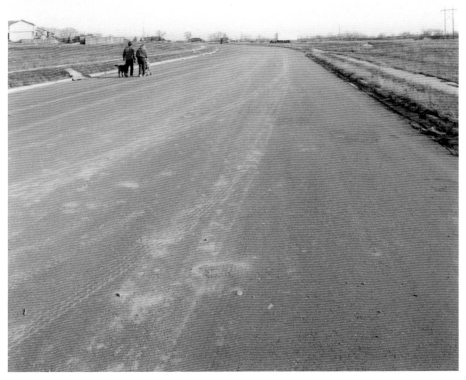

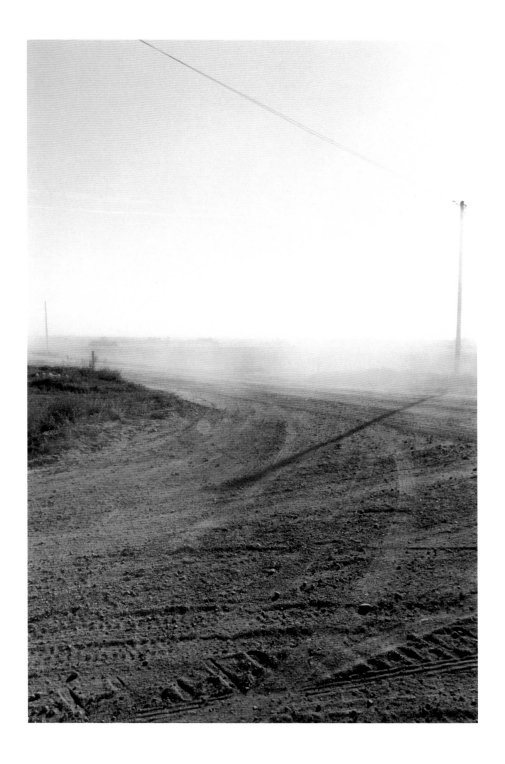

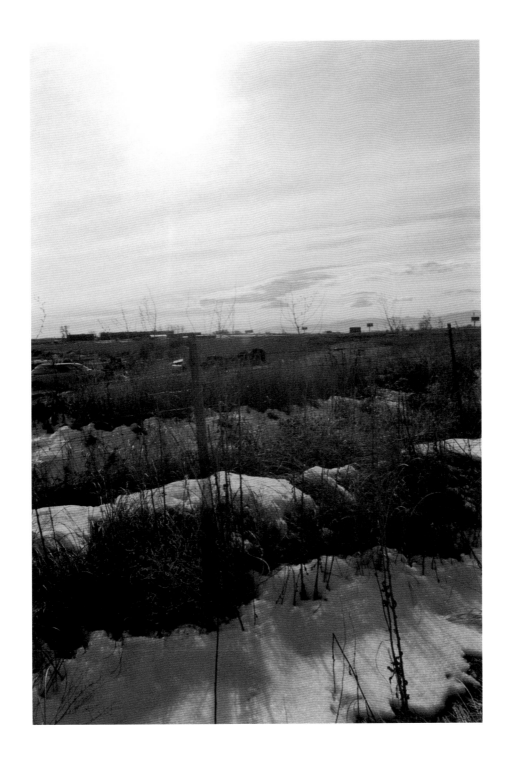

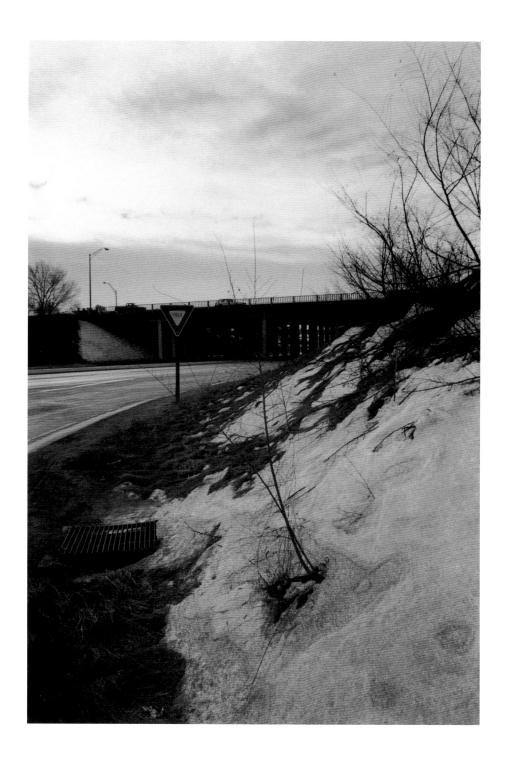

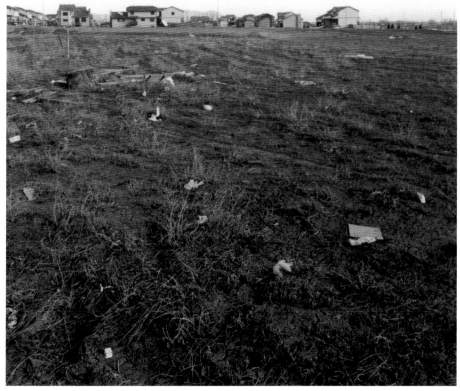

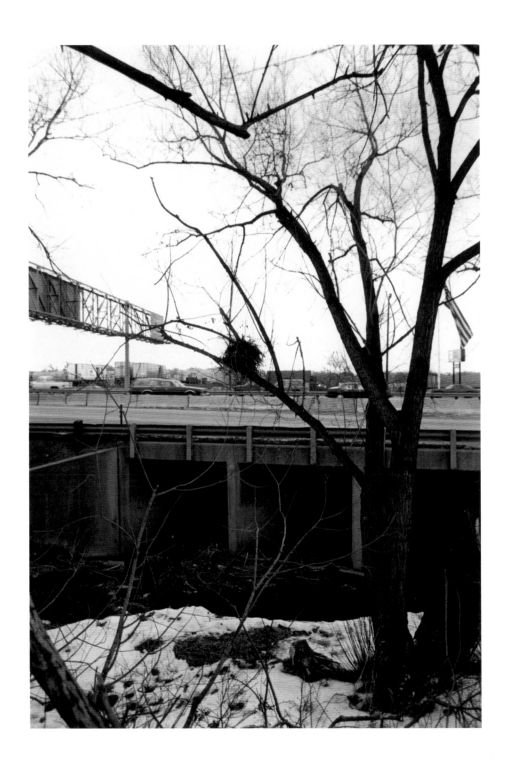

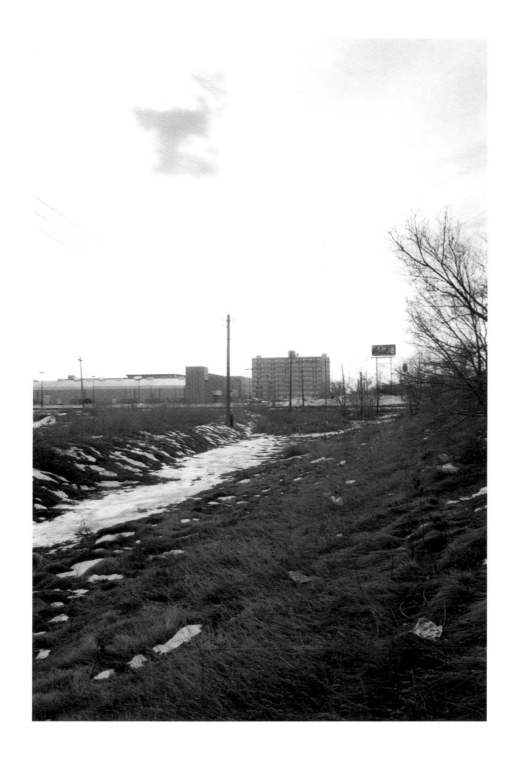

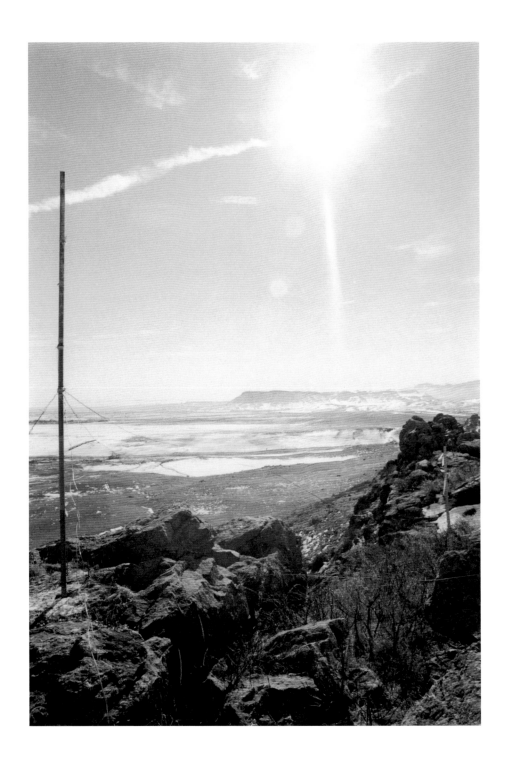

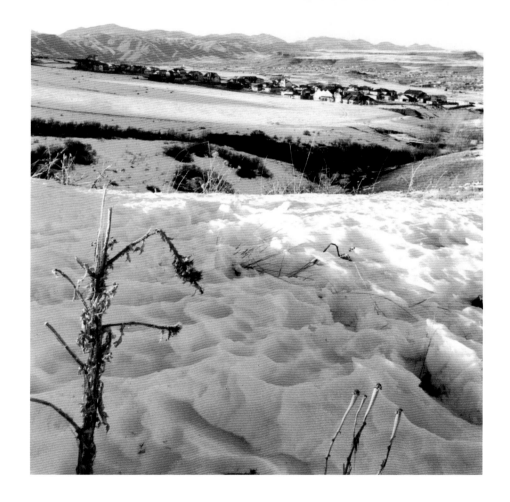

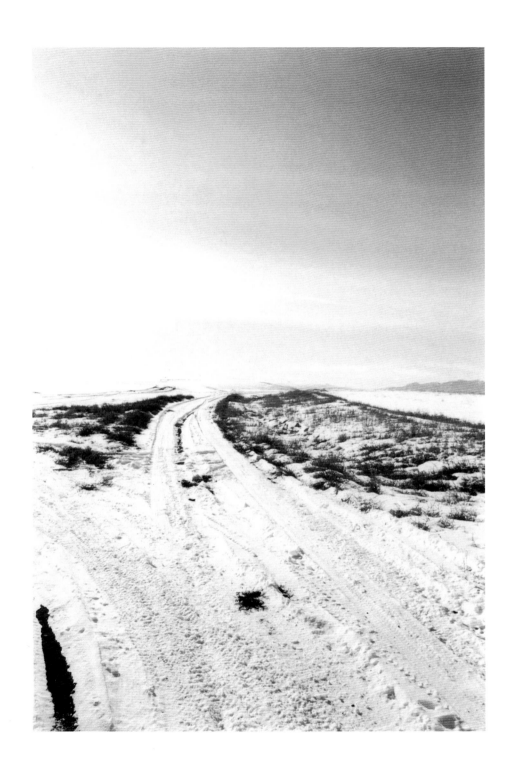

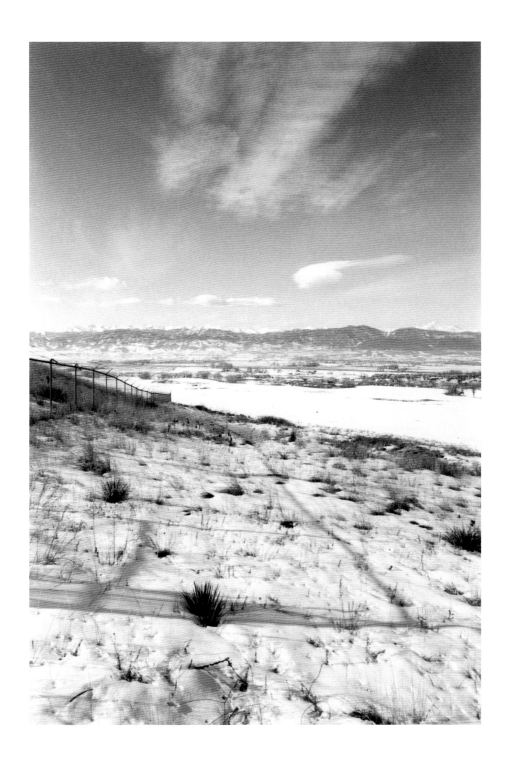

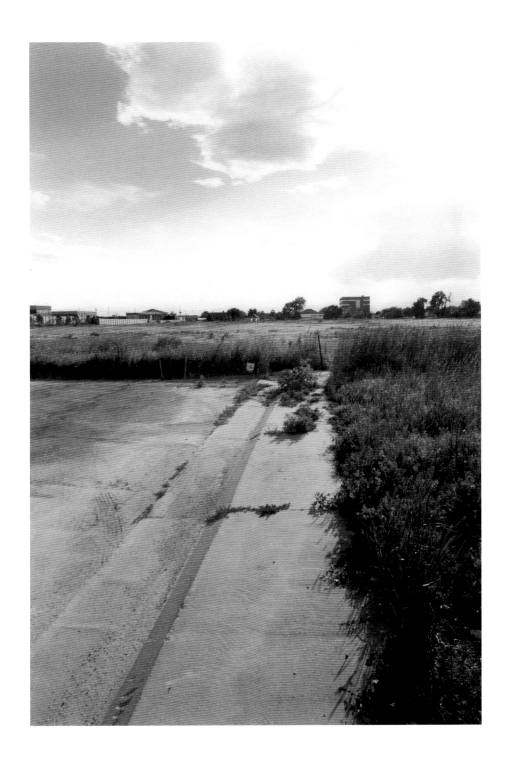

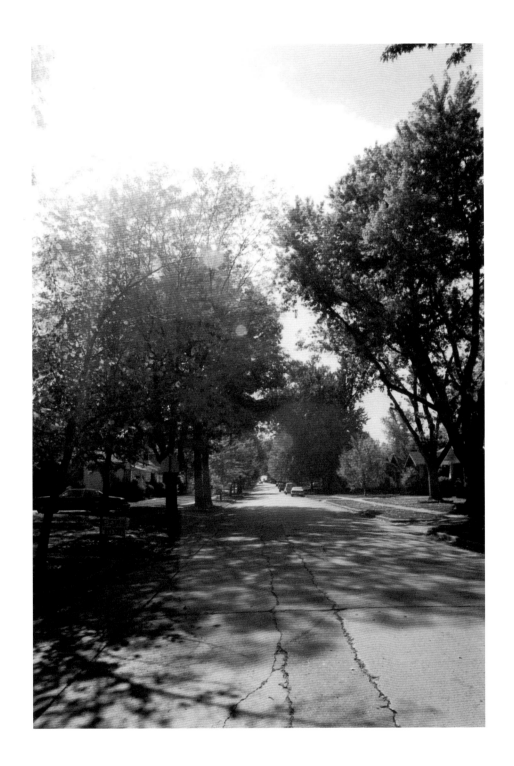

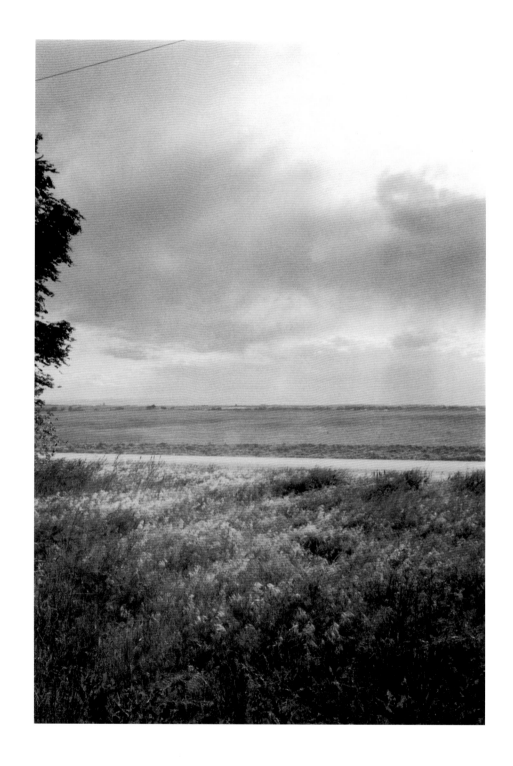

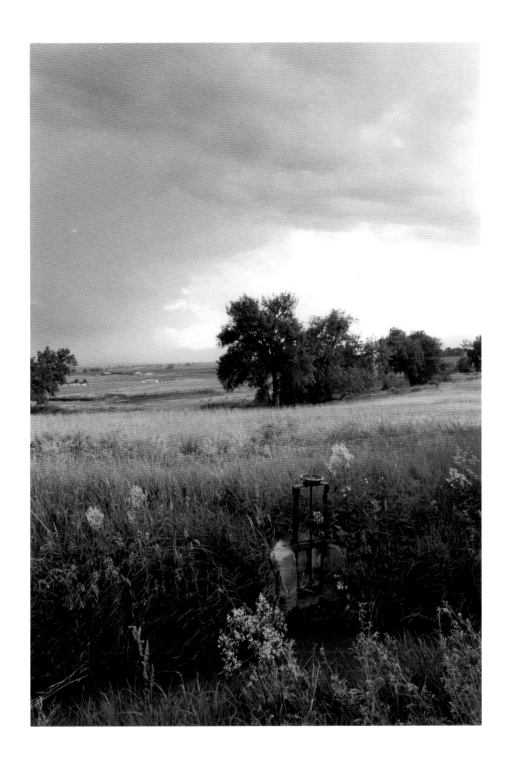

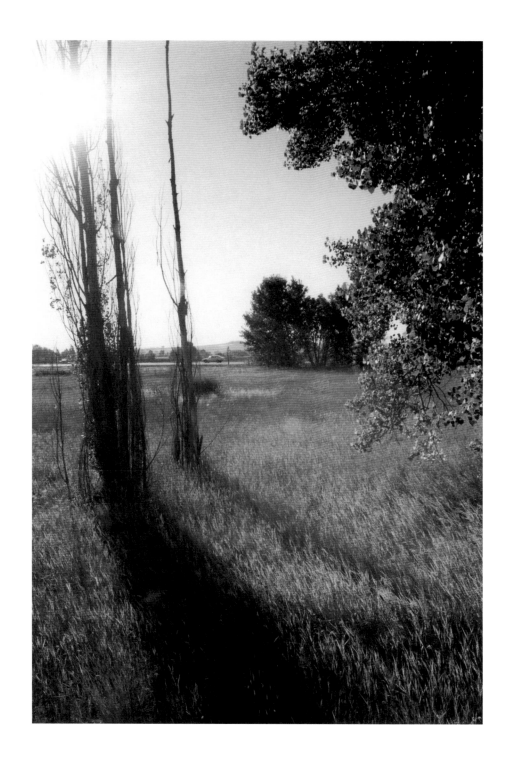

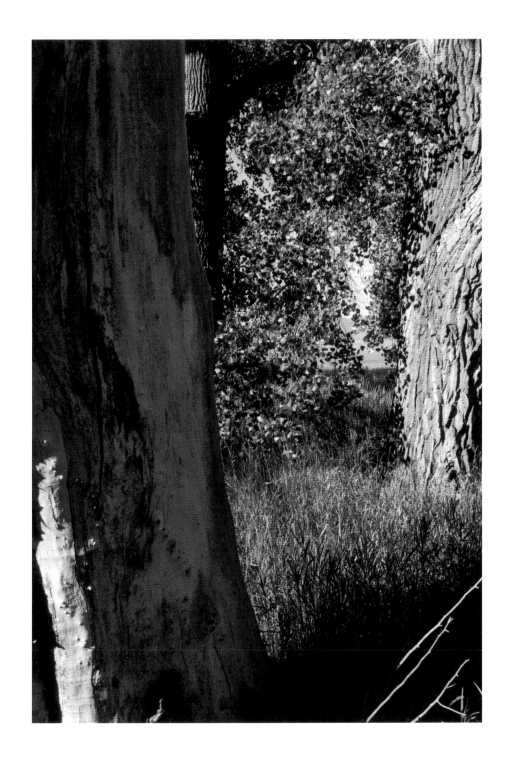

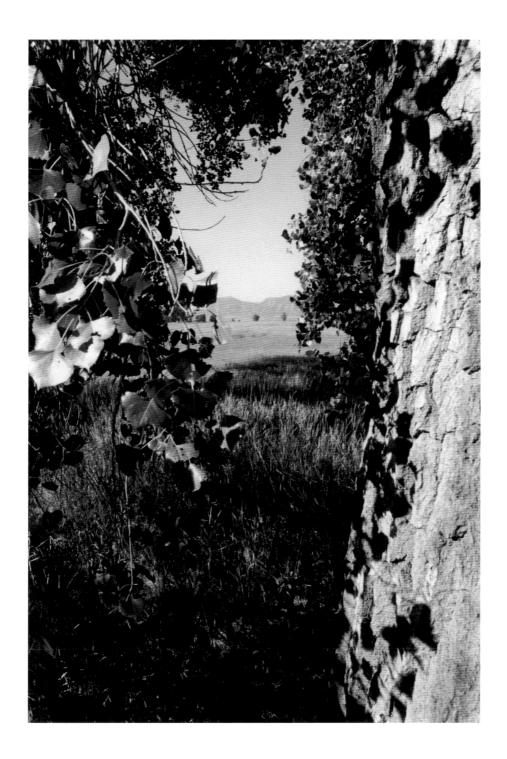

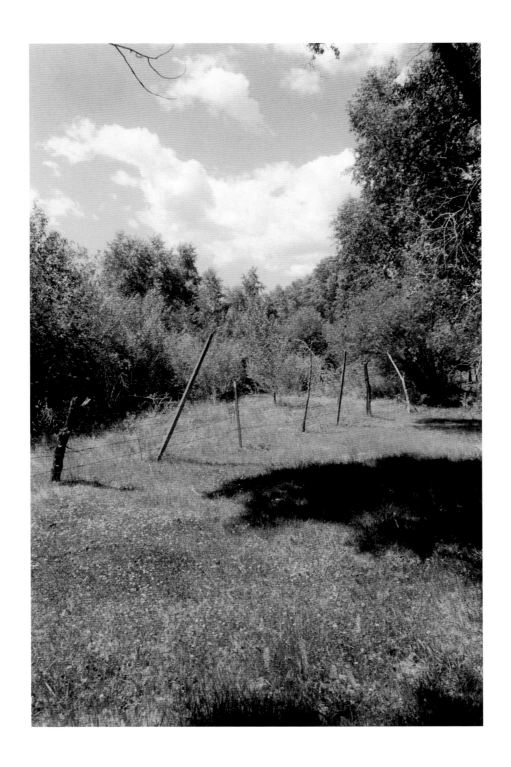

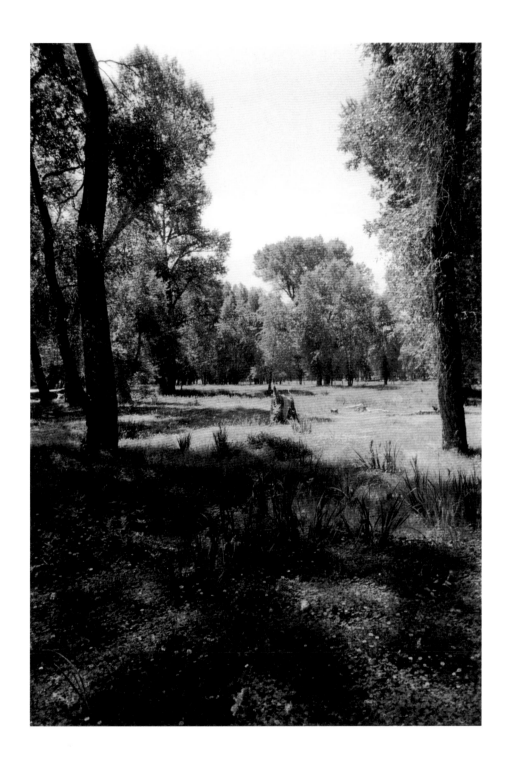

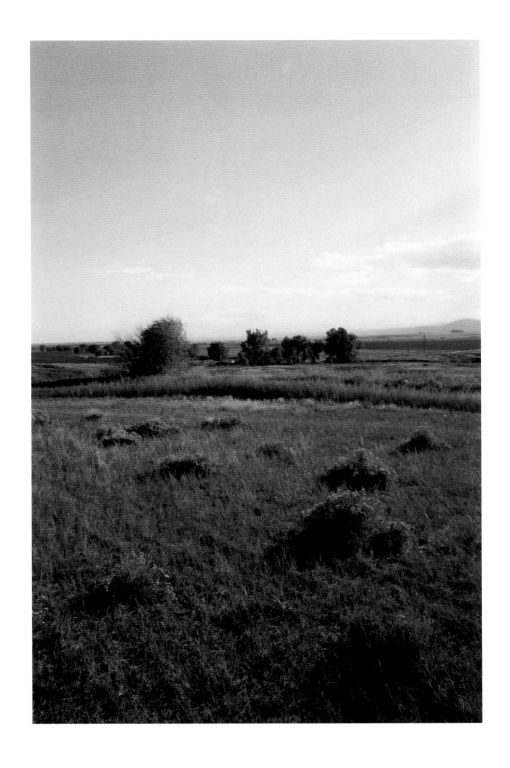

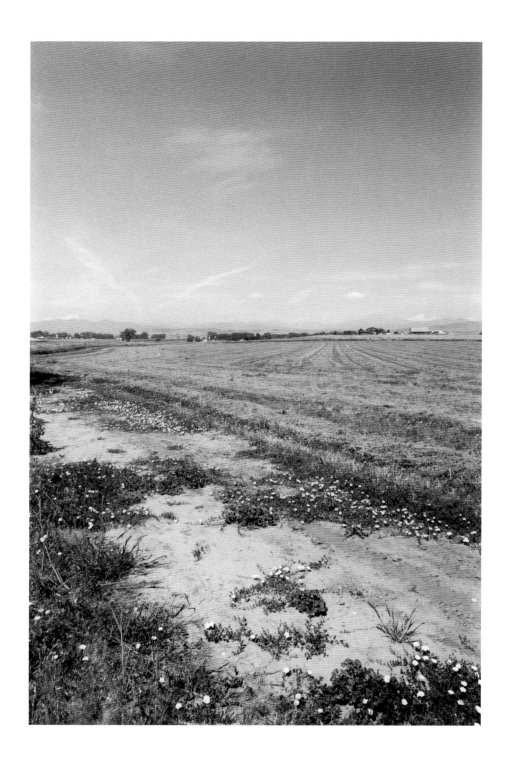

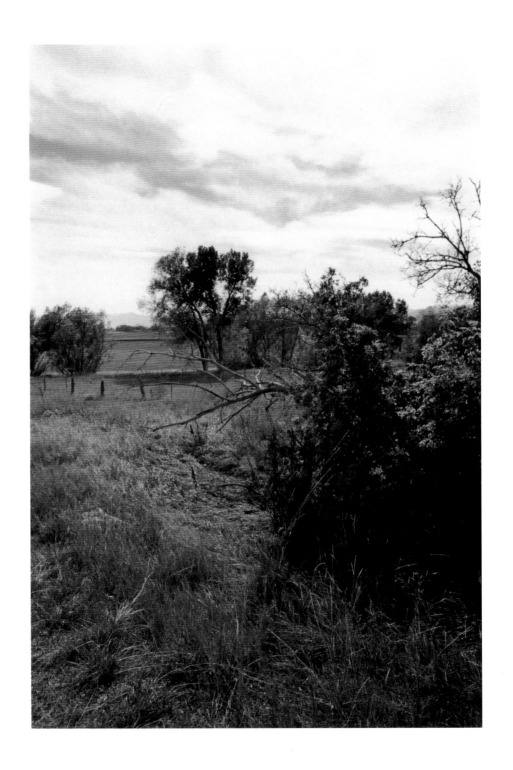

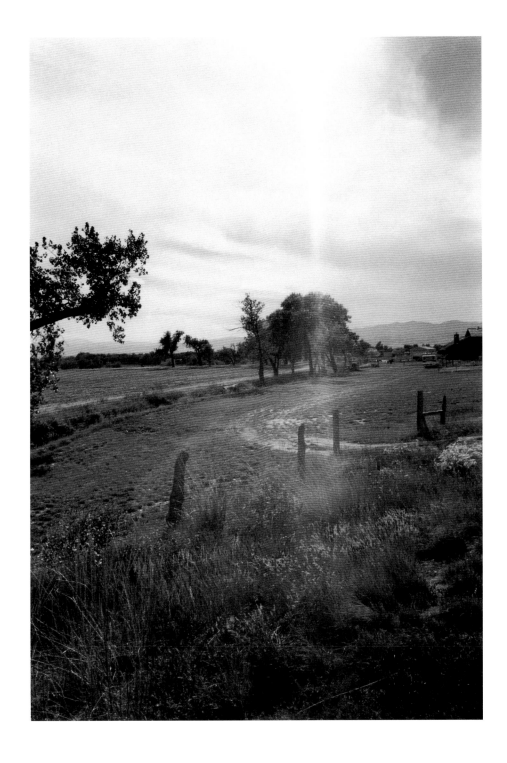

There have been evenings when the light
has turned everything silver, and like you
I have stopped at a corner and suddenly
staggered with the grace of it all: to have
inherited all this, or even the bereavement
of it...

WILLIAM STAFFORD

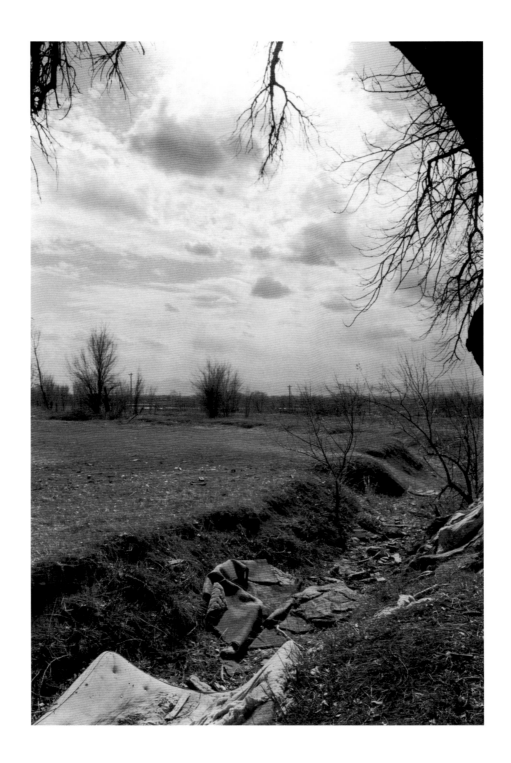

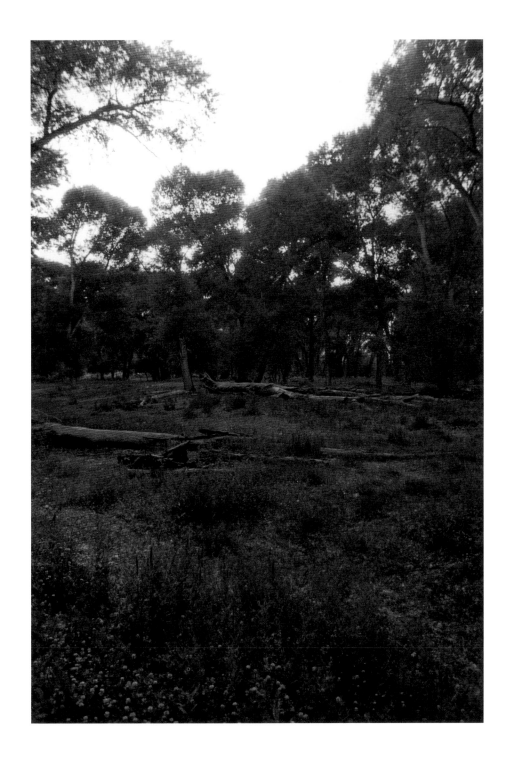

It pleases me to remember that it was Chuck Forsman who first
suggested this book and who then worked to make it possible.
We have been friends, sharing especially a commitment to the
West, for many years.

I am grateful as well to Luther Wilson and Tom Precourt for
their steady dedication to the project. And, for their generous
support, to Edwin Barber, Gene and Judy Bolles, Nancy and Gary
Carlston, Peter R. Decker, and Patricia and Jeffrey Limerick.

A fellowship from the John D. and Catherine T. MacArthur Foundation
allowed me the resources to bring things together. As Mark Twain
said, "nothing helps scenery like ham and eggs."

The pictures are reproduced through the courtesy of Fraenkel Gallery,
San Francisco, California.

Places That Will Be Saved, Old Man by the Road, and *Waiting in
Line* (pages 7 and 73) were copyrighted by William Stafford and
are reprinted through the kindness of his family and the estate.

Book design is by Catherine Mills, separations are by Robert
Hennessey, and production supervision is by Susan Medlicott.
Each is a colleague whose work I have long admired.

Printing is by Stamperia Valdonega, Verona, Italy.

©1999 by University Press of Colorado.
Photographs ©1999 by Robert Adams.

LIBRARY OF CONGRESS CATALOGING-IN-PUBLICATION DATA
Adams, Robert, 1937–
    Notes for friends: along Colorado roads/Robert Adams.
      p. cm.
    ISBN 0-87081-545-8 (pbk. alk. paper)
    1. Landscape photography—Colorado. 2. Adams, Robert,
1937– I. Title.
TR660.5.A344   1999
779'.366788—dc21   99-29077
                              CIP